The Poor Attitudes of Money (**The Fold** series,
Book 3) by Dr. Marlene Miles

Freshwater Press, 2022

ISBN: 978-1-893555-97-6

Paperback Version

Table of Contents

Dear Reader: Thank you so much for acquiring and reading this book. I pray it has blessed and enlarged you. May you soon see increases from your sowing that will cause you to marvel in the wonderment of God.

The Poor Attitudes
of Money

Freshwater

Freshwater Press

The Poor Attitudes of Money

The Beatitudes is a beautiful picture of many things, prosperity being one of them, beginning at Mark 5:3. Jesus is teaching who is blessed and what are the benefits of being blessed. Blessed means prosperous. Blessed means favored of God. As the Beatitudes repeats what is blessed and who is blessed, we get clear knowledge of what is also *profitable*. In this series, **The Fold,** we are interested in being profitable in the many ways a person can be profitable. Specifically, we are addressing finances as we look at the 30, 60, and 100-fold returns of money that is sown, as seed, in the Offering.

It is profitable for the man who is *poor*, that is meek in spirit, that is not puffed up and arrogant. It is profitable to be meek because the meek will inherit the Earth. It is profitable to hunger and thirst after righteousness because you will be filled. It is profitable to be pure in heart because you will see God. It is good to be a peacemaker because you will become a son of God. And it is blessed to be persecuted for the sake of the Gospel. There are many verses that confirm that there are rewards for that kind of persecution.

Conversely, it is not profitable to be the opposite of any of those things, for example to not be meek in spirit. God confirms every Word by having said earlier in the Bible that those who have a pride in their power will suffer under hardship, and the Earth does not yield for them.

Beatitudes are the attitudes on how to *be* for prosperity, but when we see the opposite attitude working, we see poverty and lack.

Unfortunately, there is human nature, and human attitudes that counter the Beatitudes. I call these the Po' Attitudes (poor attitudes--, the Po' Attitudes of Money.

Po' attitudes of money include:

- When you decide how much money it takes to live, usually judgmentally observing other people's spending habits, you exhibit a po' attitude that will be reflected in your money's return to you.
- Always feeling as though you don't have enough.
- Always feeling as though you'll never have enough.
- Feeling hopeless--, *born this way*.
- Always feeling like the good in life is for others.
- Self-hatred, self-rejection, despising anything to everything about yourself from your physical appearance to your status in life. These attitudes cause your inner life and its negative emotions to repel money away from you.

Judge not, and you shall not be judged: condemn not, and you shall not be condemned: forgive and you shall be forgiven,

Luke 6:37).

- *They have **people** to do this job*, is another po' attitude of money. Or,

They don't pay me enough to do that.
This is pride. Pride does not reflect the servant's attitude or heart. God rejoices in the prosperity of his <u>servant</u>, (Psalms 35:27). If you don't want to serve, you're not willing. Not willing is **not profitable** as it is not cheerful.

- Acting as though you've never been anywhere or seen anything before, is a po' attitude. Money will avoid you like the plague, so, you won't embarrass money *and* God. And so you won't hurt someone, including yourself. A fool and his money are soon parted. Quoting from my book **The Spirit of Poverty**, *A fool and his money will soon party.*

- Disobedience, rebellion, and lawlessness are also po' attitudes regarding money.

- When you decide how little money you can get by on instead of establishing in your mind and soul how much it takes for you to live according to a Godly standard that you sought from God.

Thinking like that establishes an attitude in your soul that will block Heaven from doing more for you.

Your soul wields a lot of power. For example, when you decide that all it takes for a new blouse is $40, you will live in the $40 or less blouse range all your life. When you change your attitude or open your mind that a nice blouse can cost $120 or more. Then what you need to buy clothes and live on will increase; it must. You have just put a higher demand on money, and the Earth's resources. If you did so in faith, then you can expect a corresponding return. My God supplies all my needs. If there is an increase in my *needs*, there will be a corresponding increase in my life, my wallet, for my needs. Your general finances will increase as old attitudes are torn down to build new attitudes. Replace the old with new, Godly beliefs. God will see to it.

How does that happen? You're putting your budget *vibes* out there. They're with you all day long and you there you are with your spending habits and sowing habits. When you talk, you **speak** them. Your *actions* communicate them because outside of a real move of God and the sowing of a worship seed, humans invariably sow according to how much they think they need to have *left* in their purse and wallets. I don't know where that is in the Bible.

They don't sow with the *expectancy* of a return, they just give what can they spare, or won't miss until the next paycheck. God is on *their* budget, if they got a budget. Then it appears that God is at *their* mercy.

When you sow as a worship with expectancy using Wisdom, and in obedience God can move in your situation.

When your $40 price-per-blouse stronghold gets torn down, the God-on-a-budget, God-on-*my*-budget stronghold gets pulled down also. Of course, you may put up a $120. price per blouse stronghold if you don't stay flexible, but at least you're increasing. Hopefully you may be able to say, *Since my God supplies all my needs according to His riches in glory,* (Philippians 4:19), *I can choose and have anything in the Earth. The Earth is the Lord's and the fullness thereof (and therefore mine). So, n*o more saying what is the maximum you will pay for shoes or anything when you do you are limiting God again.

Disclaimer: I am not saying that we should pay as much as possible for things. Nor am I saying to pay as little as possible for things. I am saying, when the Lord is your Shepherd, you should not want, lack, need or do without anything in the Earth realm that is acceptable to you and to God.

- *We're closed.* When you habitually put up a ***Closed*** sign at your job, never offering service beyond the clock is also closing Heaven over you. When your so-called ministry is limited to Wednesday and Sundays at church, you've got a ***Closed*** sign up the rest of the Week in the rest of the places you go.

Service is power. Service to others opens Heaven.

God opened Heaven so Jesus could come down here and **serve** us. He came to serve, but in Authority and power; you really can't serve without it. That's why serving Him and others and being *sent* to **serve** is so *profitable*.

More Po' Attitudes when it comes to sowing and growing are:

- *I need this more than they do.* Po' are the greedy covetous and selfish?

- *Po' are those with impure motives.*
- *Po' are those who give for show* who are not giving out of obedience or love.
- Po' are those who do not give cheerfully in the Offering (which includes generously). Remember cheerfulness and generosity are both profitable.

Speaking of attitudes, love is a much better motive and attitude than obedience as far as motives go. But obedience is a good start. Obedience is for the spiritually immature. Baby Christians must begin with obedience. Those who are more mature will sow for more advanced reasons. Until a fuller understanding is reached, sow out of obedience. A higher and fuller understanding should be reached daily--, from glory to glory. Necessity is not an *advanced* reason to give, but it is a reason to give. You don't just give to get, and you don't give just because somebody told you to do, except for moving in obedience.

For more on why God may not be blessing you as you think He should, read my books: ***Don't Refuse Me, Lord***, and ***Let Me Have a Dollar's Worth.***

Unprofitable

This is what the LORD says—
your Redeemer, the Holy One of Israel:
"I am the LORD your God,
who teaches you what is best for you,
who directs you in the way you should go

Isaiah 48:17 NIV

I will talk about what's profitable and what's unprofitable throughout this book as it pertains to your offerings. Profitability, being profitable describes the return of the Offering, but it also means living a profitable lifestyle that will *cause* your seeds, (natural and spiritual), to increase to 30,60 and 100-fold.

Clues and keys are given throughout the Bible. Hidden prosperity secrets are revealed to the reader. If you were taking a business course to start or improve your business, you would tune in to what makes for success and profitability. Next, you would do those things. You would not do *un*profitable things, especially not the obvious things, such as not going to work, not closing deals, and the like.

Spiritually, bad economics include things such as not sowing, laziness, not reaping—not even going out the fields that are ready to be harvested. The Bible is a spiritual economics book revealing the dos and don'ts of investing seeds in the Offering. It reveals profitable or unprofitable things regarding sowing, growing and reaping spiritual, financial and even rearing natural children. These truths apply in sowing in the Offering as well as modeling a Godly lifestyle.

As you are in the process of setting a good example for your seed, (your son), doing *unprofitable* things will set a **bad** example for it and hinder its growth, as well as hinder the 30, 60 or 100-fold increase you expect to receive on your offerings, even if they are generous offerings. The size of the Offering is important, but it doesn't in and of itself guarantee a particular size, or kind of return, or any return at all for that matter.

However, you should sow enough to get God's attention. Individuals have their altars, but corporately, the Altar of Burnt Offerings, for example was a structure that was 15 feet high and 30 feet square. Can you guess why an altar had to be that large? Do you think a quarter pounder on an altar that size would get God's attention? Okay, then. Sow enough to get God's attention.

In the Old Testament, when the priest was going to make an offering, the Offerings would be substantial, powerful, amazing.

Violations in money and tangible stewardship are things such as not increasing what you already have been given, is called *unprofitable* and *wicked*, (Matthew 25). When you've been given anything from A to Z, it is your job as a steward to find out *how* to prosper it, how to make it better, how to make it **more**, and how to increase it.

When you sow, sow to get God's attention

by sowing enough to let Him know that He's got yours.

One company's TV commercial claims they don't make any number of things. They say, *We make it better.* Making it better seems profitable to me especially since it lines up with the Word. We are not the creators of the Earth; God is. We have been created and assigned stewardship, not sole creatorship. Therefore, we really don't *make* anything, we should make it **better**. That's profitability.

Similarly, you don't *make* seeds to sow in the offering, but you make them better by *sowing* them, and you make them even better after sowing by parenting your seeds. Many things in the Earth are made more powerful and reproductive once they are sown. For example, God, Word. Seeds. You didn't make any kind of seeds, but you can make them *better.* You didn't make your children, God did, but you have stewardship to make them better. Your children are your seeds, and your financial seeds--, your investments and Offerings are called *seeds.*

For unto every one that hath shall be given, and he shall have abundance; but from him that hath not shall be taken away even that which he hath and cast ye the unprofitable servant into outer darkness...
(Matt 25:29-30)

In spiritual seed-sowing class, we learn about seeds, soil, climate, seasons, atmosphere, how to plant, as well as anything else we can learn. Relatively few know very much about any of these things, but merely do what they are told at Offering time. What have you learned through experiences reading the Bible, sermons, conferences, books, or seminars about sowing and harvesting in the Offering? I'd venture to say that most who are told *when* to give don't know much else, because if they did, they wouldn't argue and how much and still end up disobeying God. Disobedience is very *unprofitable*.

That you're interested in knowing more about spiritual sowing speaks volumes to God. He will not deny you revelation, information, and Wisdom when you ask for it. Just ask. But if you're not that interested, instead doing the same things you've done for the past 5, 10, or 20 years, is a sign of where you are in your sowing and harvesting. *That* you don't ask and pursue after more knowledge and Wisdom on this matter is also an indication of your sowing status. Your goal is to learn and know what's profitable and do it, and also to know what's not profitable and don't do that. Knowledge, Wisdom and *doing* will help because your increase with God to always be at least 30, but prayerfully 60, and 100-fold.

Double Minded Sowing

Double-minded sowing is, as I have alluded to already, something like sowing in the church's Offering but buying lottery tickets on the side and making undercover trips to the casino. How about entering sweepstakes that come in the mail? Oh, you're not sending in any money because it's *no-purchase-necessary*. Does that make it right? Whether you send them money or not, the temptation to make a purchase is there today, and once they sell your name and address to other mail order places, you'll be bombarded with junk mail and catalogs. No, I'm not knocking mail order or Internet shopping, but sweepstakes is not God system of increase.

But wait a minute, you also sowed at your church--, ***and*** in the lottery? That's double minded. Which do you believe in? Both? Can't serve God and Mammon at the same time. Can't be hot and cold at the same time unless you're sick. While sick you may really be hot while feeling cold. Hands cold. Hot plus cold equals lukewarm. ***God spits lukewarm out***.

Bouncing from the Kingdom of God to *little k*, kingdom/system of the devil should be avoided by virtue of your being a tither. Tithers are disciplined. That's part of what tithing is about.

God's Kingdom on Sunday? The Devil's kingdom by Monday. That's not good, nor is it profitable. Which one are you believing in, today? Got your bets hedged? No, you don't, because you can't hedge your bets. God won't hedge a bet placed with the devil and the devil surely won't cover one made with God. For most the problem is betting, either with God or the devil. Betting is the devil's system and the system of Mammon *(Asmodeus)*.

Double mindedness is unprofitable; God says so. Double minded folk can expect to receive nothing from God, (James 1:7). The return on the giving of the double minded is zero. Double minded folks live in the zero-fold, receiving nothing.

I've already warned you about stepping out of the *Fold* or out of the Courts of the Lord is idolatrous and foolish. If you had two gardens, one was in a chaotic outdoors, like a jungle, and the other was in a lush, prospering, climate-controlled greenhouse, which one would you rather sow in? Which conditions would you rather work in? Under which conditions would you trust your harvest to be the most abundant?

Well, there are two gardens, in a sense – one is in the devil's--, it's the world and the things of the world. The other is God's. In your real life, which one are you tending, the one in the *Fold,* in God's Kingdom, or the world's Garden of Weeds?

Adam was inside the Garden of Eden, and he traded; he served the devil and got kicked out of Eden. I believe the Garden of Eden gave 100-fold return on every seed so would have taken over the world in short order if Adam and Eve had maintained their position in it and worked it.

Trying to sow in two kingdoms? Hedging your bets? Let's try it: Break a seed in half and sow it. What do you get? Nothing. Sow one half of that same seed this week and one-half next week. What will you get? Nothing. Sow one half in church and one half at the casino. What do you get when it's all said and done, tallied up and counted? Nothing.

Every motive is judged by God. Ungodly motives, especially in dealing with people, will not bless you abundantly, especially if you oppress people regarding money. Further, when you cheat in business dealings you are not only lying, but you were also practicing a form of idolatry where you are telling God that you don't trust *Him*, that you can handle this by yourself.

None of that is profitable.

Lying

In all labor, there's profit. But the talk of the lips tendeth only to penury, (Proverbs 14:23).

God talk is profitable. You can live by every Word that proceeds out of God's mouth, and every Word that God speaks performs. His Word does what He sends it to do, (Isaiah 55:9-11). When you say what God says, there has got to be profit in it, but the talk of the vain, lazy, ignorant, and overly ambitious tends to poverty--, theirs and yours, the speaker, and the hearer. Silver-tongued folk can talk almost anybody out of almost anything. Listening to just anybody talk about anything can take money out of your pocket.

How?

How many times have you ordered from television informercials? Few? Many times? And how much have these "things" you've ordered really benefited or profited you? None. Very few. Case in point.

Should he reason with unprofitable talk? Or with speeches wherewith he can do no good, (Job 15:3).

Another kind of unprofitable talk can come from folk who are not trying to talk you out of or into anything other than to believe that **they** have good sense, Wisdom, or smarts. Rambling conversations that start nowhere and go nowhere waste your time and they are unprofitable. At best, the most you can come away from a conversation like that with is entertained, at worst confused. It's just not worth it.

He that observes the wind shall not sow, (Ecclesiastes 11:4). Consider the wind of people's winded conversations. If you're sitting around listening to folk prattle on about whatever, you will never get your work done--, not the dishes washed, nor the corn in the ground. The dinner won't get on the stove, and certainly you won't get to pray for anyone, either in person, by telephone, or by intercession. Somebody's got to cut winded conversationalists off.

Especially when you have seed in the ground, you need to get busy because you have to tend to your seed with all manner of spiritual disciplines, prayer, worship, praise, sometimes fasting, reading, and attending to the Word of God. Psalm 1, which addresses standing and sitting around listening to folk talk, is all about prosperity. I don't believe that it's rude to tell another saint, *Hey, I'd love to keep talking and listening to you, but I've got seed in the ground. I've got to go minister to it.* You would certainly do that if you had a cake in the oven or a crying baby in your arms. Selah.

Running your mouth all the time is unprofitable. Gossip, slander, and lying all lead to *no profit*. No profit means no increase.

Vanity, & False Ambition

No itching ears. Only truth will prosper your seed to 100-fold return. Watching over and cultivating your sown seed, you need to know the Word of God. You need some Word to speak when attacks come your way because of your seed, attacks will come. The enemy doesn't want you to have 30, 60, or 100-fold return in your sowing. If you don't fight the enemy, it means you *agree* with him. And you fight the enemy with the Word that is Truth.

Behold, you trust in lying words that cannot profit.

(Jeremiah 7:8)

Lying words are lying words no matter who they are coming from, whether they come from a slick infomercial, a shiny, false preacher, a bogus friend, or out of your own head. Lies will not prosper.

What?!! Out of my own head, why would I lie to myself? You wouldn't, actually you shouldn't, but some people do. Further, the enemy has a *lying spirit* that has certainly been released in this Earth. Check yourself on this.

- Do you lie to people, even little white lies?
- Do you have the *correct assessment of yourself,* good or bad?
- Do you cheat on insignificant things such as the parking meter?

- Do you keep the speed limit when no one is looking?
- Would you give back too much change?

If you lie or tend to lie, you are subject to be the victim of lies yourself, and you may be under the influence or oppression of the *spirit of lying.* Like attracts like. Liars attract liars. If you use your own wiles to get people to do things, then you also will be subject to *seducing spirits* because it's **in you.** Things attract, multiply, and seek after their own *kind.*

Here are some very common lying words and phrases:

- *A ticket that costs $1.00 can easily make you a millionaire.*
- *Sweepstakes.*
- *Raffles.*
- *Luck – (The word luck is not in the Bible, except in Eccl, NET version but it means, "investment" there.*
- *Don't worry, this won't hurt a bit.*
- *Nothing is going to happen.*
- *No one will find out.*
- And et cetera.

Jacob the Deceiver stole the birthright blessing from Esau. But Jacob wasn't around to enjoy it for 21 years while he was with Laban, his father-in-law. Laban had put basically the same moves on Jacob that Jacob had put on his brother, Esau. Jacob **attracted** what was *in* him.

Rachel stole her father, Laban's idols, from his house when Jacob, both his wives, children and handmaidens finally left Laban. Rachel was Jacob's favorite; Jacob was attracted *to* and attracted what was *in* him. So here's Jacob the descendant of Abraham, working for 14 years to marry a woman that didn't even serve God, but instead was an idol worshipper. Unless, of course, she was only going to use those idols as a back up in case Jacob's God didn't deliver.

The fact that Rachel took her father's idols explains her barrenness for all those years.

Some years later, Jacob lost his favorite wife, Rachel. So, what would you say of Jacob's prosperity and success up to that point? Like Jacob, man must stop lying because it hinders prosperity.

If you resist the devil, he will flee from you, but some devils only come out by prayer and fasting. Become vigilant to rid yourself of a *lying spirit* if you have become victim to, or host of it or other evil spirits, so your Godly seeds will multiply and bring profit and good success to you.

Gossip

Gossip can be mostly true, partly true, or even all true. Gossip can be all lies; it varies. If *lying* is at all in you, you may **believe** things that are untrue. If what you hear is not of good report. Having virtue, being true, and lovely, then it is best not to think on those things or speak on those things, (Philippians 4:8).

Gossip is very unprofitable.

Gossip is witchcraft because it's usually negative. Who gossips by saying, *Child, you won't believe it, Markus finished his doctorate and is now a full professor at Yale University?* That's not even juicy unless you have a crush on Markus.

Gossip is usually negative. At best it is harmless, but that's not why God would warn us not to be a gossip. So, the next problem might be that gossip is blind witchcraft. Gossip can repeat lies, sow discord, and cast spells. It can invite demonic influence over the person being gossiped about. I mean, really--, who gossips about *themselves*? Gossipers are always talking about the person who is NOT in the room, on the call, or in the conversation--, casting spells. Casting negative words, situations, and scenarios on them. Judging and deciding if that was good or bad, right, or wrong and in essence inviting judgement into the absent person's life.

Then, sentencing them – deciding what <u>you</u> think must or should happen to them for violating what **<u>you've</u>** decided is so wrong or grievous.

Gossip is a heinously poor attitude and action toward people; it impacts your finances negatively, and is totally unprofitable.

In all labor, there's profit. But the talk of the lips tendeth only to penury, (Proverbs 14:23).

Bound

Whatever you bind on Earth shall be bound in heaven. Whatever you *loose*, (Matthew 18:18) on Earth is *loosed* in Heaven. Is your money *loosed*? How does money get loosed in the Earth? Tithing and generous offerings, amongst other things.

Consider a bundle of seed wrapped and tied. Simple enough, it is bound. Until it is unbound will remain bound. If your seed is bound, the desired effects and results of the seed will be bound. If seed is bound in Earth, it is bound in Heaven. Haggai 2:19 speaks of the seed still being in the barn and that it hasn't *brought forth*. That means it has not reached a time of harvest. Of course, it can't *bring forth* if it's not even planted yet.

That's also why you can't stay home and have church. You have to be *loosed* first, provided you are a person who is not homebound by physical or medical limitation. Stop being bound in the house and get *loosed* into your local sanctuary. Once you're **established** there, you cannot just stay in church and do real *Kingdom* work. You can do <u>church work</u> there, but Kingdom work happens outside of the church building.

Religion substitutes church work for Kingdom work, but God doesn't.

When speaking of binding and *loosing*, most of the time we talk about **speaking**, using binding or *loosing* words as in spiritual warfare type prayers. True enough, but your Godly or ungodly **actions**, are binding and *loosing* things in the Earth and correspondingly in Heaven all day long. Your discipline in performing the disciplines of Praise, Worship, Fasting, Tithing, and Sowing in Offerings, as well as obedience and service in one-another ministry, sharing your Fruit of the Spirit, and so on are also *binding and loosing*.

You do those things all day, and all night, even while you are asleep. You're binding and *loosing* 24/7. Your words bind and *loose* and that is very powerful and effective when you think of doing it what--, 10 minutes to an hour at a time? When you purpose to do it, you bind and loose. But even when you are not consciously doing it, you are binding and *loosing* by your words *and actions* all day and probably half the night, all month, and all year, all your life.

Prove it.

I'd love to.

You can sin in any number of ways without speaking a word. Depending on the sin, you just *loosed* any number of negative influences into your life, and by sinning, you just bound your blessings from ever getting to you, all completely nonverbally. You didn't speak a word.

Your body is the temple of the Holy Spirit, (1 Corinthians 6:19). What are you watching on TV? What you're letting into your ear gates, eye gates, and all the other *gates* of your temple is of great concern. Whatever you let in will try to set up an altar. Whatever altars are in you directly correlates to the worship that comes out of you. When demonic things are allowed in, they set up their altars. Demonic spirits love to be worshipped.

That's how they grow in strength. Sinning is demonic worship.

For example, if you keep letting violence in by watching it on television, the *violence altar* that is set up on the inside of you will seek to see it more, think about it and then *do it*. Watching it incessantly builds up a faith for it. Faith when it is fully grown will **ACT**. It will *do* something.

Putting anything before your eyes and ears, looking at it, thinking about it *is* worship. You may get hooked on it; that is, you get faith for it. Then you may want to join a boxing gym. Next, a martial arts class. Later, you may enter into a fighting competition. After a while, your child who is watching this stuff with or without your knowledge, will get into fights at school. How did this happen? I just told you.

You may say nothing is wrong with that. It's only exercise. True, all things in balance and moderation. But when you get obsessed about it or saturate in it, that's another thing. You may agree that it's only make-believe--, it's just TV or a movie. It's fake. Maybe it is, but your subconscious doesn't know that it's fake. This is how people get deceived.

What you are looking at is **very real to your brain**. Your brain doesn't know the difference between real and not real, Only your soul and spirit know that, but further, your *child's* soul and spirit is not nearly as developed as yours. That's why you're always having to tell your children the simplest things. They don't always *get it* until they are more mature. Once matured, if they have been taught properly, they shouldn't want to see it, think on it *ad nauseam*, or do it to disaster. But right now, they are still <u>children</u>.

So, you argue that violence isn't bad, it's only entertainment. Maybe it isn't if you *loose* a violent spirit or create a *harmless* **violence altar** in your *temple* because you believe you're so advanced, so wise, and you don't mind lying to yourself, telling yourself that you're able to keep your spirit and soul from worshipping at that *violence altar*.

Yeah, right.

How many times a day do you think on it? That's worship. How many supplies do you buy to support it? That's also worship. You may think you're disciplined and self-willed enough to know not to be affected by the entertainment you've just experienced. No one is immune to what they look at, think about, or hear about on a regular basis. It's going to get in there. Once it's in there, only deliverance will get it out. And, that's not a one and done all the time. It can take years to get the wrong stuff out of you that you've let in. For example, alcoholics. Smokers. Drug addicts. Sex addicts. Porn addicts…

Furthermore, Wisdom, the ability to use knowledge, is based on what we let in through our eyes and ears. If our eyes, ears and minds are clogged and cluttered with devil junk, when do we have a chance to be filled with the Spirit of God, or Wisdom, so we can live a victorious life?

Instead, you could you have spent that time building a prosperity altar in your mind that would be working to drop 30, 60, to 100-fold returns to you from the Offerings that you sow in.

I remind you, that you've got seed in the ground. How is watching violence, tending to or cultivating your seed? Violence, **which is war**, tells seeds to **stop growing** because you have to go fight and there will be no one there to tend to or harvest them.

War and poverty go together unless you're making guns, ammo, tanks, or harvesting spoils.

Hint: There are no spoils in TV, movies, video, Internet, or any type of media war. They're just imaginary wars, you argue, yes, with imaginary-- **<u>no spoils</u>**. Imaginary spoils won't line your pockets, buy the groceries, pay rent, or build the Kingdom. Again, the warning here is that your soul (mind) doesn't know the difference between a real war and a fake one.

Conversely, peace and prosperity go together. Get peaceful in your spirit and watch your seeds prosper.

Or have you just orphaned your offerings by *detaching* from them so you could go play? Have you just sent your offering out to prosper with no tending, no parenting? Have you sent your seed out? Where? There--, while you relax and amuse yourself. If part of yourself is at the movies, fights, or beach, not having given God a thought, no wonder your seeds are not prospering. You can't use God like a money duplicator, throwing Him a few dollars here and there while you go do what you want, asking God to multiply your money for you. That could be why your sowing is not working. No wonder you're still not receiving 30, 60, or 100-fold. You're not still poor are you? You're distracted. Distraction will not parent, minister to, or foster a 30, 60 or 100-fold return in Offerings.

I am not saying don't ever take a break or go on vacation, but this kind of behavior habitually is rather brazen and causes your seed to be bound. Maybe you sowed it, but it is bound, stuck in that place between out of your hand and becoming a seedling that will mature to harvest. If you haven't ministered to it, then it is dormant, if God is merciful and gracious, toward you. Or, the converse, it could be dead if God just let the natural consequences of your inaction take place.

All of your life is dynamic, ever-moving, ever-changing. Who is to say what has happened to some seed that you've completely ignored while you did whatever you wanted? Don't think it's in suspended animation awaiting your return to minister to them. Put a few corn seeds in the ground. Ignore them for a year, or two. What do you think you'd have? Nothing.

Have you been ignoring seeds after sacrificing and sowing them? In the natural how much would an ignored child prosper? If you were making an Old Testament sacrifice, you'd stay at the sacrificial service until the *entire offering* is received and consumed, then go away expecting from God. The Old Testament people did.

Speaking of negative altars, you may be one to saturate in soap operas. Men see the shortcomings of women who build soap opera altars in their *temples*. Women see how men overdo it with the wrestling and boxing. Women are help mates, so men, listen to your helpmates. Women should especially be good at recognizing this because they've been deceived by looking on the **wrong stuff** before. The devil tempted Eve, telling her to *look at* that tree. Eve got an up-close and personal experience at looking and erring. Adam was disobedient. The two genders should help one another.

Soap opera (queens) watchers have *motherless offerings* out there while they feed and worship their emotions, instead of worshipping God who can multiply Seed, and bless folks mightily.

But the Word says that I have to count my seed as dead after I sow it. Good point. I used to think that was literal. Yes, counting seed as dead means don't repent of ever having sown it; that aborts the sowing process. It is as though you dig up that seed or dig the plant up. Depends on when you repent of it. And to what level it's grown in the natural. You wouldn't do that unless something unforeseen distracted you, *like a war*. If you don't dig it up, but leave off tending, it is as though you *orphan* it. You wouldn't orphan an apple tree that you planted, would you? Unless there was an emergency, then don't orphan your spiritual seeds that you have sown in the Offering. Spiritually, you've got to manage your life so that you don't have *wars* in your sowing and growing seasons. That's one of the main reasons why you need a shepherd.

More on this in the book, **Do Not Orphan Your Seed** by this author.

Covered or Buried?

The way you *cover* your seed is reflected not only in your relationship with God, but also in your attitude about sowing and money. It is shown in the way that you use money, think about money, and spend money. For example, if you see a bill and get hysterical because it's a bill. This may show that you haven't prospered much in your soul, and you don't have much faith in God. Especially if you have a job, just calm down and pay the bill.

Your seed should be covered. But it can be over-*covered*, that is **buried** in any number of ways. In this example, it was buried by emotions. Earlier, I said that a seed could be buried by flesh, especially if your sin life is not in *remission* --, as it should be.

Every time you get alarmed over money. Whether you owe it, or it's owed to you, you send a message to your brain that money scares you and that you are full of fear concerning it. When you open a letter or statement (bill), your brain doesn't know if the number written on it, $10,785.29 is coming *to you* or is expected to come *from* you.

(Is the violence real or fake?) Your brain doesn't know. All your soul knows is that when you saw that number you became alarmed and fearful. To protect you (from yourself) your soul or your emotions will set up a money stronghold to keep you from being so alarmed again. It will try to protect you from having to see numbers like that again or often, and that might mean that you repel 100-fold return on a generous offering you sowed in last month.

It may mean that you reroute a 60-fold return that was coming to you from the seed you sowed last week, never to be seen again. That might mean that the 30-fold return on the Offering just sowed for yesterday isn't coming to you because the stronghold in your mind can't handle those kinds of numbers. You can handle the low-end numbers, but not the increase.

Wow, are you paying attention? Chances are that you have a large-number stronghold if you don't sow large amounts. You sow one dollar, $5 on a good day and you go all the way up to $10 just to see what will happen. That doesn't seem very generous to the average person or God, but it's generous to you because you have a *stronghold* in this area. People call it cheap. It's a stronghold.

The results of a money stronghold, (emotional or intellectual) may mean that even though you finally have your own business, you may not do a lot of business because your mind cannot handle seeing large numbers with dollar signs, commas, or decimals in them. It may mean that as you work for someone else (for a salary or wage), you won't draw money or business opportunities for that enterprise because of **your** money stronghold. If you are a cashier, for example, you may be afraid, even apologetic to give people their totals, or their checks if you are a waitress and the bill is what *you* consider high. You are NOT a Collector and should not be in a job where you have to collect money. You will not be an asset to that company.

Also, this stronghold will stop you from asking for a good wage, or increases, or raises for yourself. I'm serious. If you're afraid of money, afraid of numbers, especially large numbers, you may *repel* money and generous returns from coming to you personally, and repel increase everywhere you go, work, and in everything you touch. If most or everyone is like you in your church, then the corporate return level of which I spoke earlier will be very low.

Some people think it's wrong to talk about money. They think it's ungodly or not Christian-like. My concern is that those people have money strongholds because Jesus talked about and taught about money often.

The policy of checking peoples' credit and backgrounds tends to pay off for banks and institutions that deal in money. Hopefully this is not to discriminate *against* anyone, but it screens out those with money blocks in their minds. It lends itself to success, prosperity, and profitability. A person with good credit who pays their bills on time, and has regular savings and investments is probably less likely to steal money in the natural. Allow me to take this deeper. That same person will also have no, to few hang ups about money.

Even if this prescreened employee doesn't *attract* money to your business, they are relaxed enough about money to **not repel it** from your business or investments, depending on in what capacity they work for you. This is why I'm so particular about who touches any of my money--, from bank tellers to investment specialists. This is one of the reasons why I try not to hire people who *work for money*.

See my book, entitled **Don't Work for Money** it is part of the **Don't Refuse Me, Lord** series.

The Midas Touch from childhood fables--, everything he touched turned to gold meant that King Midas did not have a money blockage. In his mind, there was no stronghold freaking him out when he saw large numbers on pages or large sums of money, as in gold. He had other problems, but that wasn't one of them.

One day in my dental practice, a patient paid his bill. The balance was around $7000. It had been $12,000. My novice assistant immediately began to rejoice as if it were Christmas, Thanksgiving, and his birthday, right in front of the patient. I don't think he'd ever seen a $7000. check before. Knowing the patient had contracted for over $12,000 worth of dental work, I, after counting up the cost, **expected** to be paid $12,000 all at once, but two payments was fine. When the patient paid me, I wasn't surprised. My assistant shouldn't have been surprised either because the contract had been made. I was embarrassed for my staff member and hoped it didn't make a bad impression on my office.

Yes, I was thankful and grateful, but I also had worked for it, expected it, earned it, and deserved it. I didn't need to get emotional over money. That money has responsibility tied to it. Businesses have overhead, supplies and staff, for example. Further, this wasn't miracle money, or a surprise gift. It was owed for services rendered.

I had both tithed and sown in my church's Offering, so I expected financial increase to get to me in some way. Often, it is your job, paycheck, bonuses, etc... I had worked for the $7000 that grew in my field of blessings, so it didn't surprise me. Over emotionality in this case may have set up a large number stronghold in my soul. It could have affected that harvest but may have **buried** my next seed. Balance is very important.

Now, if money comes to me that I'm not expecting, and I determine that it is from God and accept it, that might be very thrilling, and my emotions might get a little fired up. But I've got so much seed in the ground, (and so do you), that I could harvest every day, in faith, with confidence, and still not lose the wonderment of God.

Room to Receive It

If you sow properly in your lifetime, your children and your *children's* children should be able to benefit from your financial faith works. In other words, even if you live to be 150 years old, there may not be enough **room** or *time* enough to *receive* it all in your lifetime.

Jesus told the Disciples, rejoice not that the *spirits* are subject to you, but that your name is written in Heaven, (Luke 10:20). Don't marvel at the money, the money is *subject* to you, but rejoice and worship God that you're **saved**. Don't get overly excited about the money. Jesus told His Disciples, don't marvel that the demons are subject to you; but that your name is written in The Book. Same principle: Don't marvel about the money, but that 30-fold, 60-fold, and 100-fold returns come to you and prove you are a child of God, and your name is also written in The Book. You are in Covenant with the Most Holy God.

Strongholds are like tenacious chains and ropes, even if you want to break free of a miserly, miserable, poor, not-ever-having-anything mindset. You can't if you have a poverty and or fear stronghold as it pertains to money.

You have angels that obey the voice of the Lord God. Do you have God's Spirit in you? Yes. Then you have Angels that obey *your* voice too--, as you speak the Word of God.

Oh, you're not saved and don't have God's Spirit in you? Then you have angels from *the other side* who obey what you say. Either way, you have angels that do your bidding based on how much faith is released when your binding and *loosing* words and actions are released in the Earth 24/7. Your binding and *loosing* are dependent on your thoughts, attitude, knowledge, understanding, and faith. I'm serious.

Don't think I'm making this up; I'm not. The Word says that your angels don't know, can't tell, would not, and can't change what you say, do, or react to it. If you even take the Word in vain, speaking idle words, they are required by spiritual law to try to make happen what you just spoke.

Usually when you have an alarming reaction to something. you will **speak**. You *will* speak. Whenever you are not saying what God says, you are provoking Him. The Israelites, in the Wilderness were in harm's way when they provoked God's Angel, (Exodus 23:21). When you provoke God concerning your sowing and seed, your seed becomes at risk. If God can be merciful to you, He may allow a *return* on that seed, but it probably won't be a hundredfold. The return may fall down to zero. It depends on you and so many factors, statutes, laws, disciplines and precepts, as well as your attitude and many other things that are interconnected, as you are learning in this book.

So, there are so many motives and attitudes about money that cause increase to come, or to not come to you. Decrease may happen to you financially. And you may be putting many poor attitudes about money, whether you speak them or not, out there unawares. You are binding and losing 24/7.

Brazen

And I will break the pride of your power, and I will make your heaven as iron. And your earth is brass, (Leviticus 26:19).

Receiving revelation is a sign that you have a right spiritual hookup with God. It is a sign that Heaven is open over you. When Heaven is open the blessings can flow and the 30, 60 and 100-fold return can be yours. In the Bible, all kinds of things from ladders, sheets, doves, and even Jesus moved from *one dimension* to the other, from Heaven to Earth. That can only happen with an open Heaven.

When Jacob, wrestling with the Angel, declared that he would not let the Angel go until he blessed him, that is a lesson. Firstly, if an Angel came down to Jacob that meant that the Heaven over Jacob was already open. That's the first step. Who opened it? God, the Angel? Abraham? Isaac? The tithe? The Offering sacrifices? Yes, probably all of the above.

Secondly, Jacob had to *speak*, ask for, or declare what he wanted, what he needed from God. The tithe opens Heaven--, the windows of Heaven. Your declaration that you intend and expect to be blessed is the act of giving a name to your offering **and** ministering to it. The Offering says to God. *I will not let go until you bless me. I'm sowing the seed as a memorial. **I'm** going to remember it. I won't stop thinking about it and what it should bring me at fullness. I won't let go until the full harvest manifests. I won't let go until You bless me.*

As well, the Offering is the opportunity to speak to, and **name your seed**. Declaring what you want from your seed is done in the process of **naming it**. Speak something like this over your seed. *I give, so it is given unto me. Pressed down, shaken together, and running over.*

Declare what you expect. Keep declaring your expectancy until you get it. Declare what you expect to be accomplished by saying the seed's

name. Don't let go of your seed until it blesses you. God blesses you because of it, and with it. Don't let your seed go. It will *become* what you've named it.

You must live under an open Heaven for the Holy Spirit to keep you, teach you, guide you, bless you, and give you revelation. The Holy Spirit travels and communicates in more than one dimension. Heaven must be open for the blessings of God to flow into your life. Receiving revelation from God is an indication that the Holy Spirit is active in your life, and you are set for 30, 60, or 100-fold return in your giving--, as long as you do what you're supposed to do.

How does money, how can an Offering do that? Money gets your attention in the Earth, doesn't it? Money makes and seals, deals and contracts. When you put money in God's hands, the place of **multiplication**, it gets His attention in the heavens, not because it's money, but because of what money *represents* to Him. To God your money represents **your life** and God deals in spirits, souls, blood, and **life**. Anyone who gives their life will gain. Anyone who gives a part of their life will gain.

Jesus gave His life and look at all He had spiritually on Earth and now.

Exchanging money in the Earth creates contracts because people see money as money; they see it as power. Money is power, but it is the lowest power of all. *(Topic of another book.)*

Contracts (covenants) are created with God with **money** because God sees money as *life. And God deals in spirits, souls, blood, and life.* Once you get God's attention, He sees that you are really, really serious. You enter into Covenant or contract with Him. As He receives your Offering seed, and since His Word says 30, 60 and 100-fold according to your faith and *other* things, then God becomes obligated to bless you. If you think of God as a businessman or an investment banker, if the rates on the brochure, sign, or prospectus are 30, 60, or 100-fold, then it is. God is faithful.

Thirty, 60, or 100-fold is according to *your faith*, because you know He is going to deliver.

Deliver what? We already know *what*? Deliver where?

If Heaven over you is not open, how can your *return* even get to you?

It won't.

Your spiritual address, what was that again? *Which* Court? People who live at your particular spiritual address are found doing ***what***? Nomads don't reap because they haven't sown, and they haven't cultivated their seed/crop. You must **Live** somewhere that God delivers to, for God will deliver to you. If you don't stay in one place long enough, where will He deliver anything at all to you? Additionally in the hostile world in which we live, we need a *delivery anointing* to receive our abundant harvests.

(See the Chapter, ***Delivery Charges Apply,*** in **The Fold**, Book 1.)

Though I speak with the tongues of men and of angels, and have not charity, I am become a sounding brass or a tinkling cymbal,

(1 Corinthians 13:1)

You can get as deep and spiritual as you want, more spiritual than a Pharisee. You can speak in tongues, day and night. But if you don't have love, you are as a sounding brass. Imagine a closed Heaven where prayers and offerings are going up *toward* God but crashing into the iron heaven overhead instead of ascending to the

Throne of God. A sounding brass, or a tinkling cymbal --that's what it must sound like to the angels when Heaven over folks is closed. Imagine the sound of that discord in the ears of God.

If your child had instruments to make sounds and music but was not using them correctly, if they were making, instead irritating noises, you'd either try to help them play, stop them if they wouldn't, or couldn't, or throw the whole thing out. Maybe, like tinnitus, which I wouldn't wish on anyone, you'd try to tune it out and ignore it.

When we are not using our money correctly that we are receiving from sowing, no wonder we may not have God's attention. If we are not living right, walking by the Spirit, if we don't have love, our prayers may sound like clanging cymbals to God. He may have tuned us out, after a time. I'd prefer to think of God as most merciful, and ever try to help us, even if the noise is getting on His Holy nerves.

Let us walk in love so that we don't displease God.

Your 30, 60, and 100-fold harvests have to travel to you **inter-dimensionally** from Heaven to

Earth. And you need to be at the address where God expects to find you, and that is in the Courts of the Lord and in the right horizontal relationship with the other sheep of the *Fold* for the harvest to be *received*. Again, inter-dimensionally means that Heaven over you needs to be open, not closed, or brazen.

Division

Un-**multiplication**, a word I just made-up, is really **division**. Turning off **Multiplication**, not being fruitful, is bad, because it is the opposite of what God said in Genesis. God said, ***Be fruitful and multiply***. Turning off **Multiplication**, as we just discussed in the last chapter, is bad enough, but when Division is turned on, and especially in light of your sowing, you've got problems.

Division follows the *spirit of division.* In our understanding of binding and loosing, think of the *spirit of division* as in a container, like water in a glass. When you pour water out of a glass, dividing it up, you don't know where it's going. Spirits are released into the air and they're invisible. How much less do you know where a *spirit* which is airborne will go once you've let it out or *loosed* it.

Division is when two or more people, factions, or sides disagree about the Vision. The Vision is from God; *di*-Vision is not. Division in the church affects the *corporate return* of your church. The works of the flesh include sedition. Seditions means *division*, (Galatians 5:19). The *spirit of division's*, strongman is jealousy. Almost half of the works of the flesh stem from jealousy, anger, division, strife, rage, murder, etc. So, the Vision is to stay in the spirit, whereas *di*-Vision is to walk after the flesh. When jealousy is poured out of the glass, or let out of the bag, division leaks or flows out as well. And who can say where it will go when *loosed* or let out?

Earlier we confirmed that sex sins and sins of money, especially other people's money, turn off **Multiplication**. Those very same sins turn *on* Division. Having intimacy outside of covenant is either caused **by** the *spirit of division* or the sex act introduces Division into situations. Division may be the very reason why your seeds are not multiplying and prospering to maturity.

What is the solution?

Getting rid of division in order to reach multiplication is the same as having to turn off poverty to get prosperity or wealth.

From poverty to wealth, normalcy must first be reached.

Being in *division* is equivalent to being in poverty. There's no way you can get **to** wealth until you get away ***from*** poverty and begin to be **normal**. For example, being fat, waiting to be skinny, there's a stage where you are not fat or skinny, but normal.

In marriage, when you allow *division*, you can expect the return of your *fold* to decrease, diminish, or completely dry up as you move as far away from multiplication as possible. Now, it is possible that when you break up with the person that God told you not to be with in the first place, that your financial condition will improve immediately, greatly, and noticeably. I've had that happen to me. But I am mostly talking about breakups, divorces, et cetera that are the breaking of Godly Covenant.

Anyone or anything that does not promote a couple *as a couple* is an instrument or agent of division. Anyone who likes one member of a marriage but not the other is a weapon of the enemy against the marriage.

A divisive person should be shunned and avoided. I don't care if it's your friend, a family member, even your own mother, (Romans, 16:17). The devil will use anyone he can. The devil hates marriage and Covenant because Godly marriages produce Godly children.

Any relationship that you cannot have in front of and with your spouse is a potential instrument of division. Anyone who dishonors or disrespects your spouse doesn't need to be around either one of you. It doesn't matter how long you've known them when you marry.

Many times, after marriage, people's friends must change. Charles Stanley, author of *Walking Wisely*, suggests that married men should only have male friends, married women only female friends to avoid temptation, I agree, but that is not enough. Neither a man nor a woman should have a friend that does not respect and offer support toward each and both as a couple, no matter what gender their friend is. Friends who habitually pull one member of a marriage away, leaving the other home alone are not friends. They are instruments of division on assignment from the devil. When division comes, the relationship will suffer, but before then, the increase in their sowing will be greatly diminished or completely cancelled.

In marriages, *Division* is why many couples do not have children. Sometimes that division is so insidious that neither party may suspect *spirit spouse* is the cause of it! No multiplication is bad enough, but division is the opposite extreme, and it's disastrous. The *spirit of division* is also why marriages break up. When divorce comes, division is raging. Division is un-**multiplication**. It does not prosper anyone except divorce lawyers. Could this be why so many get so broke getting divorced? Division un-prospers people; it is UN-**multiplication**.

Division gets let out of the bag as early as the childhood playground with cries such as, "The boys against the girls!" Where is that in the Bible? And who can say where *Division* will go once let out? Guard your life, guard your Christian walk, marriage, covenant relationships and you will guard **Multiplication**, staying in the Fold of 30, 60, and 100-fold increase.

What Cha Doin'?

*Half a nation changed their gods, which are yet no
gods. But my people have changed their glory for
that which still not profit, (Jeremiah 2:11).*

As said before, illegal covenants and soul
ties lead to idolatry. Ignorance leads to idolatry.
Man will worship *something*; man was made to
worship. He's supposed to be worshipping God,
but the devil perverts everything he can.

Desperation leads to idolatry. The *Just* live
by Faith, not in desperation. The *Just* are not
idolaters because Faith circumvents desperation.
Ignorance of God's laws, leading to idolatry is the
natural course of the sin-nature of man. And, as
stated before, sexual sin leads to idolatry. Sin, in

general, whether or not that sin is idolatry will lead to the sin of idolatry.

Idolatry is *unprofitable* because idols cannot come into the *Fold*, and you must be one of the *Fold* to sow a seed that is *received*. Idols cannot come into any part of the Outer, Inner Court or the Holy of Holies, so you cannot go into any of these places *with* idols, either. The profitable lifestyle is in the *Fold*, that is in the Courts of the Lord. Unprofitability is *outside* the Fold and the Courts of the Lord.

Where You *At*?

You never leave the *Fold* or the Courts of the Lord to go play with idols. If you do leave, you won't get your hand stamped as though you're leaving in amusement park and coming right back. You leave the Courts of the Lord at your own risk. You may not get back in at all, or things may not be the same as you left it when you come back.

Seriously, if you are really experiencing the presence of the Lord, why would you want to leave?

If you are sowing for profit or increase, you need to be in the *Fold*, in the Courts of the Lord. Spiritually you need to stay where you sowed so you can check on your fields and harvest. So, if you're *in there*, why leave? A farmer wouldn't walk away from a field that he has seeded, except to check another.

No one has anything sown in the idol *god's* field other than weeds and corruption. So, there's no reason to leave God's Field. Anyone who thinks so is double minded.

Idolatry is consuming, and distracting folks from entering into the presence of God and tending to their fields and seeds. Since idol worship is considered evil behavior, the term, *wicked* gets attached to it. When you go to worship idols, even if it's just one, the very seeds and harvest that you're attending are left unattended. Abandoned, neglected, orphaned seed is taken away from the wicked, and laid up for the *Just*. God said so, not me, (Proverbs 13:22a). When you leave out of the *Folds* of the Courts of the Lord, no one holds your place. No one holds your seat, even if you leave your Bible in the pew.

Similarly, whatever you do that causes you to leave off tending your crops is unprofitable--, your new friend, your drugs, your car, your other money, your new idol. Whatever you do, that causes you to leave the Courts of the Lord, even if it's to go into the courts of the law, or to a court of man, diminishes your harvest. The only exception is leaving to go minister to another person; to go get souls.

Go get souls!

It's always unprofitable to leave the Courts of the Lord or the fold *without* the shepherd, or without being under authority, that is, **sent**. There are wolves out there. The Word says that he who has put his hand to the plow and turns back as not fit for the Kingdom, (Luke 9:62). When you've planted seed or begun the process of preparing to plant it, but then turn back, leave off from doing it, leave out of the presence or the relationship with God, there is no harvest for you. The Word says that you are not fit, (Luke 9:62). This implies that there is no Grace, and surely no Grace is unprofitable.

Jesus was full of Grace. We know that Jesus had an *excellent Spirit*, and He was very profitable. Jesus was so profitable that He could sow seeds and reap fish. He could sow Words and reap men. Jesus was so excellent of Spirit and profitable that He could sow and reap bread; He could even reap an abundance of fish on dry land. Jesus was so excellent with His mo' better (more excellent) ministry that He sowed Himself and reaped brethren for the Kingdom.

Are you *called* to leave the Courts of the Lord? Grace and anointing are given when you are *sent*. When you are *sent* it is with purpose and in authority. The Holy Spirit goes with you when you are *sent,* and you will never be left alone or forsaken.

Don't just leave, but first prepare, and wait to be *sent*; that's where the prosperity is.

Grieving Authority

I'm Telling--,

And You're Going to Get It, Or Maybe You Won't

Obey them that have rule over you and submit yourselves for they watch over your souls as they that must give account that they may do it with joy and not with grief, or that is unprofitable for you.

(Hebrews 13:17)

To grieve someone means to cause them great distress, discomfort, or to make them sorrowful or afflicted with sadness. It means to offend them and often it is related to the attitude by which you do or don't do something that is asked of you. In Hebrews 13:17 the word, *grief* there means a sigh or to groan. A cheerful attitude goes a long way in giving and accompanies obedience in a way that is profitable to you. Recall, anything that is profitable to you is profitable to your seed in the ground.

Grieving your pastor, leadership, any spiritual, or civil authority, is *unprofitable*, and it's really not smart. If you grieve your managers or supervisors at work, that's not profitable. If you grieve civil leaders, you may end up in civil trouble. Law enforcement people ensure civil obedience. The enforcer of Spiritual law is the Holy Spirit. He brings conviction, correction, and chastisement as necessary to those whom God loves and calls, *son*. Here, you are the son, not your sown and *received* seed.

As the son, either by birth, birthright, or adoption, you can receive in the 30, 60, and 100-fold return and offerings. You have a right to it. Hint: don't grieve your parents. Honor father and mother. Parents, do your job. Teach your children well.

As you are still parenting your seeds that you have sown, are you being a good example? Are you a good role model, as if you were actually birthing and raising a human child versus a financial harvest?

Let's talk about how authority impacts your seed. Being set under Authority is profitable.

The Centurion said to Jesus that he was a man set under authority, like Jesus. The Roman Centurion understood that authority is what made things happen. The Centurion understood that authority causes things to happen by spoken word. *Just speak the word*, he told Jesus, *and my servant will be healed.* Authority works many times by just speaking the Word. Other times it works because of your presence, or the presence of, and/or actions of your representatives.

Parents have their first and main God-given authority in the home, over the home and their minor children. I am stunned, and not in a good way, at the numbers of parents who stroll their children through grocery and department stores perched in shopping carts. The children direct as the parents push the buggies and children point and yell, Stop! The parent applies the brakes to the shopping buggy so the child can get whatever they want from the shelves, or play with, and tumble down displays. Then the child-obedient parents stroll the kids to the next aisle where they scream again, Stop! Surely these must be unsaved parents with little unsaved, cart-riding, finger-pointing, Stop-yelling, buy-me-whatever-I-want, children.

Who's in charge here?

The authority in that child-parent dynamic is tumbled long before they encountered the first blue light special display. Authority in the home and over your minor children is one of your first authority levels. When you can't manage to stay in authority in your own home over one or two small children, how do you expect to be set *in* and *under* authority over spiritual matters?

Why do you think you haven't gotten that promotion on your job after all these years? It's spiritual. It's more than spiritual, it is also natural. Do you know how misbehaved your kids are at the company and church picnic? If the boss promotes you, his kids will have to play with your kids. Oh yeah, it's natural.

Do you really think that since being under authority and being set in authority is profitable, and if you're not that, your seeds will prosper 30, 60, or 100-fold? I don't think so. If you can't exercise authority in your home in regard to your children, what are you going to do with 100-fold return in your sowing? The Bible even tells us that a man who is called to ministry, even as a Deacon should have a well-mannered home, ruling their houses and children well, (1 Timothy 3:12).

If 100-fold does somehow miraculously happen, what are you going to do with that prosperity? Have your child take it from you? Waste it on toys? Why would God prosper a person who is letting their child or children run their lives? Would you? That is the same as giving the child all that money. God doesn't do that. God had a begotten Child; Jesus was His name. Jesus was set under Authority. If Jesus, then your children as well.

Jesus sent the Word, and the Centurion's servant was healed, 100% healed, not 30, not 60, but 100% healed that same hour, because of decency, order and being set under Authority.

Your lack of prosperity is not because God is not **able.** Authority is related to Dominion, Dominion to spoils, and spoils to prosperity. Dominion can't happen if you don't have Authority. The amount, 100% healed and the time, same hour speaks of Jesus and the man's faith who was standing in the gap for the servant. The servant may have known that the Centurion was seeking Jesus for his healing, so the healing may have been dependent on the servant's faith, as well and any in the household who knew of the Centurion's plan. Could have--, but it was based primarily on Authority, which was the lesson's object.

My parents had full Authority in a house with ten children, and it wasn't by violence. Violence in the home is usually a sign that there is no Authority held by those who should be in charge.

Mutiny by children is usually by force or violence. However, some children can charm their parents into or out of anything, using guilt, fear, pity, sympathy, and other modes of witchcraft. Yes, it is emotional manipulation, and that's witchcraft. Un-prospered souls only know power as force. Violence is physical force. Witchcraft is a force; witchcraft is spiritual violence. Witchcraft, which compares to the sin of rebellion, is extremely unprofitable; you should not let your child practice it at all, and especially not on you, (1 Samuel 15:23).

Parents who have been too slack for too long find that violence is the sequela to frustration either from them or toward them.

I remember how hard it was to let go of the concept that it was all about me and that everything I wanted I should get. Being born into a very large family, I had to arrive at that understanding very early in life. It is much easier learned earlier than later. If I truly wanted something, I had to get it myself, for myself. Growing up meant I had to understand that, not have offense, unforgiveness, bitterness, or a bad attitude about whatever I did not get. It also meant not to covet the stuff that I didn't get or worship the things that I did receive or acquire.

This is helping someone.

If you still have bitterness, deep hurt, and other bad emotions, especially over childhood disappointments, you are not prospering in your soul. It was hard for me, and I was never a shopping cart child. I never had many toys, things, or stuff. So how hard do you think it is for overindulged children to get over the concept that it ain't all about them and that they have to grow up, be accountable, reasonable and responsible someday? Probably very difficult. In the worst cases, children like these never get it. They are the ones who turn on their parents, steal from them, lie to them, or run away because they are not having their way. You've heard about kids who have mutinied Authority, erupting in violence, inflicting bodily harm when their servant-parents are not, cannot, or will no longer serve them the way they want.

Even if the parents are no longer *able* to serve the kids--, the kids and the parents are all too old. Bitterness, resentment, hostility, and animosity set into the spoiled child's heart and soul. What is that run-over parent going to do with 100-fold return in his giving? Try to appease that monster that they've created by overindulging the child, and withholding discipline, calling it love?

Not walking in your Authority is unprofitable and it affects the *return* of your offerings.

The church's Authority in the Earth, shows up as the pastor's job is to report on church and Christian behavior at judgment, which will be a reflection of your souls' prosperity. But before then your behavior is told to God and that report affects the *Fold* of the *return* of your sowing as the child's behavior should affect their allowance. Think of your behavior and your *Fold* of blessing. Do they correlate?

Think of your return levels as your allowance from God.

Curse not the king, no not in thy thought; and curse not the rich in thy bedchamber: for a bird of the air shall carry the voice, and that which hath wings shall tell the matter. (Ecclesiastes 10:20).

Now God knows about a response you just had to a certain situation. Did you buck authority? Who told? A little birdie, and you are going to get it --, or maybe you won't. Maybe you will get nothing. But when good reports get to God, you will see a 30-fold increase. When the better reports get to God, 60-fold. When your best reports get to Him, you are at a 100-fold increase.

However, a bad, *but true,* unprofitable report equals zero-fold.

Little Oppressors

As for my people, children are their oppressors,

(Isaiah 31:12 a)

In the name of love, parents create their own oppressors, as much the same as they create their own *idols*--, their children. It usually starts at childbirth, when parents become captive with the small life form that God has given them. If they at all worship the child, they move further into captivity. A child, even a baby is smart enough to realize that they are ruling the roost. The child loves this power and may begin to wish to rule and reign in the house. Childish charm can turn to teenage terror when overindulging the child has gone on too long or gone too far.

We train a wild animal before you love it. I'm not calling your child and animal. But in the animal world, love without discipline gets you scratched, bitten, or mauled.

A child's soul has not begun to mature. A non-prospered soul cannot handle being worshipped. Lucifer was not prospered in his soul, and he wasn't even being worshipped. He was only **near** the worship. Lucifer was delusional. That was God's worship, not his. The immature and un-prospered soul can't handle being worshipped. Don't worship children or an un-prospered soul. It creates monsters. Oh, solve the whole thing--, only worship God.

Satan's imps and minions are just like him immature, but wanting to be served, obeyed, and worshipped like so many spoiled children. Authority in the hands of the spoiled and immature is viewed as power to them, and it is usually misused or abused.

If God gave and gave before we prospered in our souls, what kind of planet would He be trying to run? Right now, people will be running amok with power, and on ego trips. We do see some ego trips, but power belongs to God. God didn't indulge Jesus. Jesus had boundaries and parameters in which to minister. There were things Jesus did not *want* to do, but He submitted to God. Example: Gethsemane.

God didn't have Mary and Joseph pushing Jesus around in a shopping cart at the Walmart, letting Him pick out everything He wanted every weekend. Jesus could have been a very spoiled child, teenager, adult. And He would have no ministry. We would have no salvation. Thank God for Jesus and His soul prosperity, which serves as a substitution for our sin-sick souls and even now as an example to us all.

Help your children by setting Godly order in the home from the beginning. Do your children a favor, treat them as God treats us. Levels of authority, responsibility, and benefits come with soul prosperity, (3 John 2).

Teach your child to respect you. Disrespecting parents is the way children fall under the Curse of the Law, succumbing to poverty, sickness, and maybe even eternal death. Disrespecting parents is *unprofitable*. Respect is not natural in a child; they have to be taught. Some children have to be made to respect adults and authority, but it will benefit them and strengthen their life.

When you don't establish Authority in the home:

1. Your child won't respect you.
2. Your child won't understand Authority in or out of the home.

    a. Church authority,

    b. Civil authority.

3. Your *return* in your Offerings will be negatively affected.

4. You and or your children are subject to live in poverty, sickness, and eternal death.

Children should not curse their parents.

What?

Children say bad things about their parents?

Oh yeah, what children?

Spoiled children who do not understand when discipline finally has to come because they have been getting their way since the egg and the sperm united. Or worse, children who have unfortunate lives because they don't realize that everyone in the world is not going to treat them like babies or as the king of the world as their

82

parents do, and subsequently cannot make it in the real world.

What kind of children? Children who grow up to be teenagers and adults who have things happen to them because they were never disciplined. So, they lose out financially, socially, and/or physically, blaming their parents for letting them have their way all the time and never preparing them.

Such as?

The pregnant teen. Whose parents taught her about sex, but she never learned that when **they** said, *No*, or *Don't*, they meant it. They were inconsistent and yielding where they should have been consistent and firm. She could talk them into and out of anything. She didn't respect their Authority because she didn't learn Authority under their parenting model.

Such as the young man whose 3rd illegal drunk drag racing accident leaving him maimed for life. His devotedly religious parents taught him about alcohol and the sins of drinking, but he was never disciplined. He was never disciplined to understand, No, Don't and Authority. A child who never respected his parents because they let him have his way 24/7. He didn't have to respect Authority at home, so drinking, driving, speeding, breaking civil authority meant nothing to him. When the child is not taught, authority, you don't model it for them or walk in it yourself, your child will end up like you.

When people disrespect Authority in the natural, they end up with diminished returns in Offerings, as well (if they even go to church). Folks with Authority challenges don't go to church, or don't stay in a church long enough to be planted.

Whatever problems your disobedient and rebellious child brings home, all of their life, will be your problem. A child who does not respect authority will bring home the harvest of corruption, so it won't just hurt them, it will hurt you too, eventually.

Whether at home or church, if you are or were such a child or member--, repent.

IMPORTANT: I am in no way attempting to be cold hearted, disrespectful or judgmental to the parent(s) who have disciplined, taught and raised their child (children) to the very best of their ability, but one or more of their children just seem self-willed, or stubborn like they are cut from another whole cloth. Children like that can be a real challenge and just won't learn or want to learn things the hard way. That is really a *thing*, and it can be so frustrating to the parents, the whole family, actually.

One rebellious child can destroy a lot of good and a lot of family unity.

Also, I am not disregarding the presence of foundational and/or ancestral altars that are a reality in everyone's life – to the negative or the positive. To the blessing of having more godliness in your nature and in your life, versus having more hardships, and having to deal with curses in life. Ancestral altars are not the parents' fault, neither are they the fault of the child. Sometimes one child may be selected or singled out, it seems and no matter what the parent(s) do, it seems like an uphill struggle. I am not judging that and would like to discuss what to do in that case in another book that is yet unwritten and untitled.

Great Cloud of Witnesses

The Book of Hebrews talks about a great cloud of witnesses. Many times, I've seen things that seem as though they can't be any of my business. I have felt that I was called to be a witness, of sorts, and without even asking to be one. Many times, I feel as though I might have enjoyed my day better if I had not have seen some of what I've seen in my life. I probably needed to see it, to pray and intercede and tell it, if asked by God--, to be a witness.

Bless those in authority over you.

I try to behave in a manner that I believe God, the Holy Spirit in some innocent witness who may have to be the informant of me on any matter at any time, might find hopefully pleasing, but at least unobjectionable. It keeps me trying harder, knowing that matters concerning me are given in reports to the *king* and that those reports affect or effect the *return* of my sowing. I'm very serious and sober about my lifestyle. Not the *appearance* of it, but my **real** lifestyle. Reports are given to the *king* by any number of birdies, or ministering spirits.

The devil is the accuser of the brethren, but the Blood covers our sins. Jesus imputes to us His righteousness, and God gives ample Mercy, and Grace sufficient. God loves you in spite of your humanity. Have you noticed that when you do something good a corresponding blessing seems to come? Those *reports* are how God can supply vengeance when you've been wronged so you don't have to. His *ministering spirits* have already apprised Him of the choices you've made and the behavior you've exhibited. When the good, better, and best reports get to God, you're going to get it--, some 30, some 60, and some 100-fold.

Not being set under Authority is unprofitable to the return levels of your harvests.

Do you know any of this?

Wisdom does.

Dear Reader: Thank you so much for acquiring and reading this book. I pray it has blessed and enlarged you. May you soon see increases from your sowing that will cause you to marvel in the wonderment of God.

Dr. Marlene Miles

The Books in this series

THE FOLD, Receiving 30, 60, and 100-Fold

https://a.co/d/hJpjRc2

Name Your Seed, (Book 2) https://a.co/d/busdf5r

The Poor Attitudes of Money (Book 3)

https://a.co/d/28yla9L

Do Not Orphan Your Seed (Book 4)

https://a.co/d/6q9bRnS

Power Money: Nine Times the Tithe is

a powerful prequel. https://a.co/d/7L14seL

Mini Books: **When the Devourer is Rebuked** https://a.co/d/8JqsSCL

Let Me Have a Dollar's Worth

https://a.co/d/7TW8qFZ

Also: **got Money**?

https://a.co/d/h1bpU8V

The Spirit of Poverty

https://a.co/d/dV6njEg

Prayers Against the Spirit of Poverty

https://a.co/d/aOqhKF6

My Sowing Journal is a journal to record your sowing, track the goodness of God and record your testimonies to share.

https://a.co/d/6icVIXA

Also mentioned, the **Don't Refuse Me, Lord** series, https://a.co/d/9TmGSeD

to include **Lord, Help My Debt**

https://a.co/d/3OF6IjH

& **Do Not Work for Money**.
https://a.co/d/9UGMUda

They can be read in any order and should bless you tremendously.

Christian books by this author

AK: Adventures of the Agape Kid

AMONG SOME THIEVES

Ancestral Powers

As My Soul Prospers

Behave

Churchzilla (Wanna-Be Bride of Christ)

The Coco-So-So Correct Show

Demonic Cobwebs

Demonic Time Bombs

Demons Hate Questions

Do Not Orphan Your Seed

Do Not Work for Money

Don't Refuse Me Lord

Every Evil Bird

Evil Touch

The FAT Demons

Fruit of the Womb: Prayers Against Barrenness, *Book 2*

got Money?

Let Me Have a Dollar's Worth

Living for the NOW of God

Lord, Help My Debt

Lose My Location

Made Perfect In Love

The Man Safari *(I'm Just Looking)*

Marriage Ed., *Rules of Engagement & Marriage*

Motherboard: *Key to Soul Prosperity*

Name Your Seed

Plantation Souls

The Poor Attitudes of Money

Power Money: Nine Times the Tithe

The Power of Wealth

Prayers Against Barrenness, For Success in Business and Life, *Book 1*

Seasons of Grief

Seasons of War

Second Marriage, Third Marriage any Marriage

SOULS in Captivity

Soul Prosperity: Your Health & Your Wealth

The *spirit* of Poverty

This Is *NOT* That: How to Keep Demons from Coming at You

The Throne of Grace, *Courtroom Prayers*

Warfare Prayer Against Poverty

When the Devourer is Rebuked

The Wilderness Romance (3- book series)

       The Social Wilderness

       The Sexual Wilderness

       The Spiritual Wilderness